C++ and Rust

Building High-Security, High-Performance Systems

Table of Contents

Chapter 1. Introduction

In this comprehensive Special Report, we delve into the depths of two prevalent programming languages: C and Rust. Our focus lies on how they contribute to building high-security, high-performance systems — a topic that demands attention in our increasingly digital era. Even if you're not steeply technical, we make sure to unravel this high-stakes subject with clarity, making it straightforward and accessible. We delve into the specifics of these programming languages, highlighting their unique strengths and capabilities. Whether you're a seasoned programmer looking to deepen your understanding, or a curious newcomer fascinated by the intersection of technology and security, our Special Report is designed to guide you through the intricate maze of C and Rust without overwhelming technical jargon. Embark on this enlightening exploration with us and unravel the intricate workings of these powerhouse languages.

Chapter 2. Understanding High-Security, High-Performance Systems

Systems that prioritize performance and security play vital roles in various sectors. They are key in spaces such as fintech, health tech, defense, communications, and more. Understanding the intricacies of these requirements and how different programming languages cater to them forms the basis of this chapter.

2.1. C++: The Industry Veteran

C++ is an extension of the C programming language, designed with enhanced abilities for system programming, embedded systems, and resource-constrained applications. It provides low-level functionality with user-defined types, making it efficient and convenient.

C allows for both high-level and low-level programming which affords the developer a greater amount of control over their applications. This control extends to system resources, memory management, and hardware access. Its robust nature and powerful capabilities have made C a cornerstone language across various sectors.

Security in C++ is typically managed by adhering to best practices and writing clean, error-free code. No automated memory management exists, meaning that the developer is responsible with handling pointers and allocating or deallocating memory. This forms a double-edged sword: if handled correctly, it offers excellent performance; if mishandled, it leads to memory leaks and undefined behavior, presenting security vulnerabilities.

2.2. Rust: The Rising Contender

Born out of Mozilla labs, Rust was explicitly designed with the aim to offer both high-level performance and security. Eliminating common system programming pitfalls like null pointer dereferencing and buffer overflows, Rust adds extra security layers while maintaining performance.

Rust's main security feature is its unique ownership system. When a variable 'owns' memory, it is the sole entity authorized to free it. This eliminates double freeing of memory and null pointer issues. When ownership is transferred, Rust ensures that no dangling pointers result from this operation.

Another crucial Rust feature is its concurrency model that prevents data races. It enforces these constraints at compile-time, which brings down the number of runtime bugs and unforeseen security breaches.

2.3. Performance Comparison

Both C and Rust promise high performance, but they approach this goal in different ways. C provides direct access to hardware and low-level resources, along with direct memory management, leading to efficient and typically speedy performance. However, these benefits come with the risks of potential programming mistakes that may not only affect performance but also lead to serious security consequences.

Rust aims to provide the same level of performance but does so while enforcing strict memory safety rules. The handling of these responsibilities by the Rust system eliminates common errors seen in C++, but the checks and balances can sometimes cause minor decreases in performance.

2.4. Security Comparison

In the realm of security, Rust holds an upper hand. Rust's ownership system, along with its strict enforcement of memory safety at the compile-time, can make it more secure against common programming mistakes, which are often the cause of security vulnerabilities.

C, on the other hand, leaves more room for such errors due to its flexible nature and lack of automated memory management. This is not to say that secure applications cannot be written in C, but it requires a greater degree of care and attention from the developer to do so.

2.5. The Right Tool for the Job

While C and Rust are each equipped with their own benefits and drawbacks, the choice between them often boils down to the specific use case. C has been around for decades, has a mature ecosystem and an extensive community, and might be the preferred choice for legacy systems or for performance-critical applications where the developer is confident in handling its pitfalls.

On the other hand, Rust is gaining traction in modern system design due to its security guarantees, especially in applications where safety is critical. Just like C++ it is also capable of low level system access, so it's a good choice for system programming tasks, though it may have learning curve for those used to C-style languages.

Understanding these systems inside out is an interesting yet complex journey. It demands patience, dedication, and a deep dive into the world of technology and security. But once accomplished, it opens up grand vistas of understanding in the realms of high-security, high-performance programming.

Chapter 3. Unpacking C++: History and Evolution

Over three decades ago, a language was conceived that would change the course of computer programming: a language characterized by rich libraries, explicit memory management, and a combination of low-level and high-level features. This language, known as C++, was derived from an earlier, simpler language, C, by a Danish computer scientist named Bjarne Stroustrup.

3.1. Birth of C++

In the late 1970s, Bjarne Stroustrup was involved in a project named C with Classes, which aimed to provide high-level features like classes and objects on top of the C programming language. The objective was to allow developers to write more human-friendly code and manage complex systems more comfortably. However, the goal was not just to create a higher-level language but to create one that did not compromise on efficiency and performance, the very essences of C.

In 1985, C with Classes developed into C, a true superset of C, which retained the powerful low-level features of its predecessor while incorporating critical high-level features. The name C signifies the increment operation in C, implying the language is a step ahead of C.

3.2. Language Progression

After the birth of C++ in 1985, the language continued to evolve, with new features being added and existing ones improved. The ability to define classes and objects was a significant leap from C, emphasizing the object-oriented programming paradigm. The incorporation of exception handling allowed to manage errors in a way that didn't derail entire programs immediately, improving the robustness and stability of software systems.

In 1998, the first standardized version, ISO C98, was introduced. This standardization marked a significant step in C evolution since the language features and syntax now had a regulatory body - the International Organization for Standardization (ISO) - ensuring the language evolved in a consistent direction. New features such as the Standard Template Library (STL), namespaces, and templates were added. The STL provides a set of common classes for C++, which includes classes for various data structures and algorithms, obscuring their complexity behind user-friendly interfaces.

3.3. Modern C++ Revolution

In the next few years, C underwent a major revolution, leading to the release of a new standardized version, C11, in 2011. C11 has since been fondly referred to as C0x because experts anticipated its release in the mid-2000s. C11 brought with it a horde of features that significantly expanded its capabilities. Auto types, lambda functions, new container classes, smart pointers, among others, graced the language. Notably, advancements also targeted the frequently criticized area of C — its complexity. The revisions aimed to make the language more user-friendly and easily adoptable.

The newly added "auto" keyword implemented type inference, thus relaxing the strict type definitions necessitated earlier. Lambda expressions simplified the process of writing short functions, thus fostering leaner code. Null pointer types were formalized, reducing errors linked to null pointer usage. Concurrency support was also enhanced, better aligning it with growing multi-core processor technology, and raising performance levels.

Following C11, the ISO released additional updates in 2014 and 2017, referred to as C14 and C++17, respectively. These updates continued to refine the language capabilities and focus on user experience. The syntax became more expressive, and several libraries received improvements. Concepts introduced in this period aimed to enable clearer declaration of requirements on template arguments, making use of the language's existing strong type checking.

The most recent C version, C20, was ratified by ISO in December 2020, and it's the most feature-rich version to date. Features like coroutines, concepts, and ranges were introduced. These bring the potential for vastly easier-to-read code, more efficient execution, and new ways of structuring logic and control flow.

3.4. Impact on the Software Landscape

C++ has remained one of the most influential programming languages for decades. It is central to vital software systems, and its low-level features contribute to system-level software and high-performance systems. The language's influence on other programming languages cannot be understated. Its Object-Oriented Programming aspects influenced numerous other programming languages, including Java and Python.

Through the years, despite criticism for its complexity, C++'s control over hardware, robust community, and powerful features have solidified its place in the industry. Though it's competing with modern languages, its compatibility, performance, and flexibility make it a consistently desirable skill in the software job market.

Overall, as we trace the historical development of C, it is evident that the language's focus on performance, efficiency, and flexibility has remained steadfast. From its birth in the early 1980s to its constant evolution throughout the decades, it shows an unwavering commitment to improving and adapting. It is thus that C continues to hold an influential position in modern software development, supporting everything from game development to high-frequency trading systems to embedded systems. Despite the advances of new languages, the rich history and continual evolution of C++ ensure its continued relevance in our increasingly digital world.

Chapter 4. Exploring C++: Core Features and Advantages

C++ is a widely sought-after language by developers all over the globe. It was devised by Bjarne Stroustrup in 1979 at Bell Labs as an extension of the C programming language, with improvements in terms of data abstraction, object-oriented programming, and generic programming.

The language has stood the test of time, and it remains as one of the most efficient, flexible, and powerful languages, especially when performance is paramount, or when precise control over memory management is required.

4.1. General Structure of C++

C is built on the skeleton of the C programming language, thus inheriting its basic syntax and most of its constructs. Just as in C, the program code of a C program is composed of functions. The primary function in any executable C++ program is named "main". Programs typically have a flow that starts with the main function and proceeds through function calls to secondary functions.

```cpp
#include<iostream>
using namespace std;

int main()
{
cout << "Hello World";
return 0;
```

```
    }
```

In programming nomenclature, '#' includes the contents of the iostream file which contains declarations of all the input-output functions in C++. These functions are part of the 'std' namespace. The main function begins its execution with the code written inside the brackets. 'cout' is used to print text onto the console.

4.2. Object-Oriented Programming

C++ brings in the concept of Object-Oriented Programming (OOP). OOP is a design methodology that revolves around data (objects), and the functions (methods) that directly interact with said data. Here, the object functions and data manipulations vary according to the object's type. This principle fosters efficient problem-solving and information cohesion.

1. **Class**: This is a blueprint for creating objects (a particular data structure), providing initial values for its state (member variables) and implementations of behaviour (member functions or methods).

2. **Object**: The instances of a class

3. **Methods**: In C++, methods are often known as member functions. These are functions defined within a class and they manipulate the object's data.

4. **Access specifiers**: In C++, 'public', 'private', and 'protected' are known as access specifiers. These define how the members (functions and variables) of a class can be accessed.

The following example demonstrates simple Class and Object creation in C++:

```
class Car {
```

```cpp
public:
    string brand;
    string model;
    int year;
};

int main() {
    Car carObj1;
    carObj1.brand = "Toyota";
    carObj1.model = "Corolla";
    carObj1.year = 2002;

    Car carObj2;
    carObj2.brand = "Ford";
    carObj2.model = "Mustang";
    carObj2.year = 1969;

    cout << carObj1.brand << " " << carObj1.model << " "
<< carObj1.year << "\n";
    cout << carObj2.brand << " " << carObj2.model << " "
<< carObj2.year << "\n";

    return 0;
}
```

4.3. Performance Efficiency

When it comes to raw computational performance, you will find few languages that can compete with C. C offers extensive control over system resources and memory. It is a statically-typed language, which means types are checked during compile-time rather than run-time, allowing the compiler to optimize most code ahead of time. Direct writing of assembly language code for processor-intensive functions is also supported.

4.4. Memory Management

In C, the engineer has tight control over memory management. This kind of control allows for significant performance gains, as the programmer can optimize their memory allocation and deallocation routines. This manual memory management can also potentially lead to issues such as memory leaks or dangling references, so be cautious when dealing with C memory management routines.

4.5. Relevance and Recency

Although C might be a well-aged language, it continues to be updated and improved with time. As of the moment, the latest revision of the C standard is C20, which continues on expanding its functionality and efficiency. C is not stuck in the past, it is a progressive and growing language.

4.6. Adaptable and Versatile

C++ will let you do whatever that you wish to do. It is remarkably flexible. It does not prevent low-level manipulations and it provides high-level abstractions if needed. It can be used for procedural programming as well as object-oriented programming.

The sheer flexibility of C++ makes it a language of choice for pretty much everything: client-side applications, server-side applications, gaming, real-time trading, embedded systems, and virtually any system where performance and precision are paramount.

4.7. Vast Community and Rich Libraries

Another great advantage of C is its long history, which means an expansive ecosystem of libraries and tools to turn to. From GUI libraries to mathematical libraries to game development frameworks — there is a C library for most needs.

Furthermore, the supportive global community of C programmers provides countless resources, problem-solving forums, and educational materials making it easier to dive into C, face and overcome challenges.

4.8. Conclusion

C is a tried and tested language. Its combination of speed, versatility, and platform independence makes it a choice of preference for high-performance software development. It is suitable for almost anything, from device drivers to artificial intelligence. With its robust and efficient toolbox, the extensive C libraries, and object-oriented features enhancing code stability and maintainability, C++ remains highly relevant in the programming world.

Chapter 5. Unveiling Rust: History and Philosophy

Rust is a powerful, high-level, performance-driven language that carries a philosophy which emphasizes safety and performance. It's relatively new, designed by Graydon Hoare at Mozilla Research, with help from the open-source community and first released in 2010.

Rust materialized from a project initiated in 2006 by Graydon Hoare, who was later backed by the emerging powerhouse, Mozilla, in 2009. The language was designed to provide developers a modern tool that allowed control over hardware, similar to C++, but with a heavier emphasis on safety. It includes baked-in concurrency and memory-safety features, including a complex system of 'ownership' for memory guarantees with zero cost abstraction.

From the onset, Rust's design philosophy centered around three fundamental domains: safety, speed, and concurrency. Incorporated into its design, Rust has proven to be a fearless, concurrent, and practical language. It's a blend of tried-and-true systems engineering languages while also leveraging innovative language design.

5.1. Birth of Rust

Graydon Hoare started working on Rust as a personal project in 2006. This was during a time when multi-core processors were becoming popular, but current languages were ill-equipped to deal with the complexities of concurrent programming and were filled with inherent risks, which gave rise to system crashes and security vulnerabilities.

In 2009, Mozilla started sponsoring the project due to its potential to solve the pervasive issue of concurrency bugs in Firefox. The intention was to rewrite components of the Firefox browser's rendering engine, Servo, in Rust, leading to safer and more parallel browsing. This move gave Rust the platform and resources it needed to develop into the language we see today. The formal announcement about the development of Rust was made in 2010 with the first alpha version going live in January 2012. After several years of iterative improvements and community feedback, Rust 1.0, the first stable release, was officially out on May 15, 2015, signaling its readiness for production use.

5.2. The Rust Philosophy

Rust's philosophy traces its roots to a design document known as 'Rust Means Never Having to Close a Socket,' written by Hoare in the early development days. The document's metaphoric title speaks to one of Rust's core guarantees: memory safety without a Garbage Collector (GC). The language is designed to help developers craft correct code without the cost usually associated with high-level languages.

In Rust, if the code compiles, it means much more than its syntax is correct – often, it means the code is logically sound as well. The compiler checks for null or dangling pointers, concurrency issues, and a host of other bugs that commonly plague C++ programs. The compiler does this without incurring runtime costs associated with traditional safety measures like GC or runtime checks.

Rust's zero-cost abstractions ensure that developers don't pay an unseen performance cost for using the language's high-level structures. The language uses static dispatch by default, allowing methods to be inline in the generated machine code, so the high-level code often performs just as well as the equivalent low-level C++ code.

The language's philosophy is reflected in how it offers control over system resources. Similar to C, Rust provides control over memory layout and includes low-level manipulations as needed. However, unlike in C, Rust operates safety even when dealing with lower-level controls.

5.3. A Focus on Concurrency

Rust was designed in an era where multi-core processors were becoming commonplace, and concurrency was moving from a niche concern to a fundamental requirement. Rust's concurrency model aims to make data races entirely impossible. It does this by using a borrow checker to enforce a concept called 'ownership.'

To Rust, the concept of memory safety is non-negotiable. The language's ownership system lays the foundation for this. Every piece of data in Rust has a particular owner, and the language's rules ensure there is only one owner at a time. Duplication or borrowing of the ownership happens following stringent rules, enabling safe concurrency.

Overall, the development, evolution, and core principles of Rust parallel the advancements in the software industry. From its humble beginnings as a personal project to being recognized as StackOverflow's 'Most Loved Language' for the past five years, Rust boldly carves out a space of its own in an otherwise crowded programming world. Rust's focus on safety and concurrency without compromising on speed has positioned it to not only augment the industry's most popular languages but also to serve as a viable alternative for application and systems programming in a high-performance, high-security world.

Chapter 6. Exploring Rust: Key Features and Strengths

Rust is a unique, performance-driven programming language that focuses on a few key areas: memory safety, concurrency, and system-level performance. Recently, it has gained traction due to its focus on "zero-cost abstractions", the notion that one can use high-level abstractions without incurring performance penalties.

6.1. Principal Features of Rust

Let's begin by probing the salient features of Rust that set it apart in modern programming.

Memory Safety: Rust's signature feature is its emphasis on memory safety, without the need for a garbage collector. It ensures safety through a system of ownership with a compiler-enforced set of rules. For programs to adhere to these rules, memory usage must be determined at compile-time instead of run-time - this eliminates common pitfalls such as null or dangling pointers.

Zero-Cost Abstractions: Rust is designed to provide the power of lower-level languages with the convenience of higher-level languages. They achieve these with 'zero cost abstractions', which essentially means that any abstraction, like a function call, class or virtual method, doesn't impose any additional runtime overhead. The belief is, there should be no penalty for abstracting, only for concrete runtime behavior.

Concurrency without Data Races: Rust addresses the complex issue of concurrency as well. Its ownership system is well-poised to eradicate many concurrency and multi-threading bugs during compile time itself.

6.2. Delving Deeper into Memory Safety

Memory safety, a primary Rust strength, demands further exploration. Rust guarantees memory safety through a system of ownership which includes features such as borrowing, slices and lifetimes.

Ownership and Borrowing: Rust's ownership model includes strict borrowing and lifetime rules, enforced at compile time, ensuring that memory is properly managed throughout the program. There's exactly one binding to any resource, and Rust enforces these rules at compile time, dramatically improving data race conditions and other concurrent processing concerns.

Lifetimes: 'Lifetimes' in Rust represent the scope for which a reference is valid. They are explicitly annotated to help the compiler verify at compile time that references will always be valid, thus eradicating a whole class of bugs related to invalid references, dangling pointers and so on.

6.3. Rust's Powerful Concurrency Model

Data races are the nemeses of concurrent programming. Rust's unique approach helps prohibit data races at runtime.

Primitive Types for Concurrency: Rust includes several core language primitives for concurrency, such as `std::thread` for spawning threads and `std::sync`, which contains concurrency primitives like atomic types and locking primitives. This makes concurrent programming a built-in, core feature.

Ownership and Thread Safety: Rust leans heavily on ownership to ensure thread safety. In Rust, the concept of ownership ensures that only one thread can mutate data at any given time, effectively eliminating data races.

6.4. Performance Considerations

While Rust focuses on safety and concurrency, it also offers system-level performance. Let's explore what gives Rust its high-performance edge.

Lean Runtime: Rust has a negligible runtime and no garbage collector. It operates on the "you don't pay for what you don't use" paradigm. Therefore, you have fine control over memory usage, cache locality, runtime polymorphism, minimal runtime, flexible interfaces, and many more low-level details.

Interoperability: Rust follows the C ABI for maximum interoperability and can be linked into any language that follows the same ABI. This means Rust's raw performance is on par with C and C++, but with more tools and safety checks.

In conclusion, Rust emerges as a force to reckon with in the contemporary programming space. It masterfully marries safety and concurrency features with high-level performance. Its unique features, zero abstraction cost, and robust memory safety, make Rust an exciting realm of exploration. As programming continues to evolve, Rust is primed to play a significant role and is certainly worth the attention of seasoned programmers and newcomers alike.

Chapter 7. In-Depth Comparison of C++ and Rust

Alright, let's dive right into our exhaustive comparison of C++ and Rust.

C++ and Rust, both highly influential languages, have left significant imprints on the software ecosystem. Despite the commonality of purpose, each offers unique characteristics and features that set them apart. In this comparative analysis, we'll delve deeply into four key areas: memory safety, performance, usability, and ecosystem.

7.1. Memory Safety

Rust was developed with a focus on memory safety without sacrificing performance. The ownership paradigm unique to Rust, helps prevent bugs resulting from memory management. A piece of data in Rust has a single owner, and the scope of the owner dictates the lifespan of the variables. Borrow and lifetime checking exist to prevent dangling pointers, and concurrency bugs are minimized via Rust's concept of immutability and atomic reference counting (Arc).

C++, on the other hand, allows more direct control over memory organization, allocation, and deallocation with the help of explicit constructors, destructors, and RAII idiom. However, incorrect usage of these features could potentially lead to major memory safety issues like memory leaks, dangling pointers, and double frees.

7.2. Performance

Performance is a critical aspect for both languages; however, the handling differs.

C shines in its ability to provide low-level access and manipulate system resources directly. It offers advanced optimization, detailed control over compilation, and inline Assembly code. Real-world performance of C is often influenced by the skill level of developers, though - the intricate control it offers often comes with complexity.

Rust, aiming to match C++'s performance, makes safety a priority. With its focus on zero-cost abstractions, it ensures safe code does not impose any performance penalties. Likewise, Rust enforces strict compile-time checks to prevent runtime errors, thus enhancing execution speed.

7.3. Usability

C has been in the industry since 1983, which grants it a mature set of tools and libraries. The language is highly flexible, offering multiple ways to solve a problem. It has a more traditional, albeit large, Standard Template Library (STL) which is performant and heavily optimized. However, C's syntax is more complex, an outcome of its rich feature set and heritage, which can be challenging for newcomers.

Rust has made a concerted effort to improve developer experience while ensuring system-level control and performance. The friendly compiler error messages, built-in package manager (Cargo), and auto-generated documentation make development smoother. However, as a relatively young language, Rust's ecosystem isn't as broad as C++'s, although it is expanding at a vigorous pace.

7.4. Ecosystem

As an established language, C++ has a rich ecosystem with an extensive range of libraries that can be leveraged for almost any kind of task. However, library acquisition isn't standardized; developers may have to hunt for dependencies across different platforms, posing potential security risks and code duplication.

Rust, with its built-in package manager Cargo, simplifies dependency management by providing a centralized location for libraries (crates). While Rust's ecosystem is not as large as C++, it is growing rapidly with quality crates that provide efficient ways of doing common tasks.

7.5. Conclusion

Choosing between C and Rust essentially boils down to specific project needs, development team experience, and future perspective. C offers more control and has a vast ecosystem, but it also demands prudent skills to maintain memory safety. Rust, in contrast, ensures memory safety, a rich typing system, and excellent development tools, at the cost of a less mature ecosystem and steeper learning curve.

Both C++, with its legacy and flexibility, and Rust, with its revolutionizing features and safety promises, are powerful contenders in the sphere of systems programming. Bridging the benefits of both could be the ideal fusion for the future generation of software, blending control, memory safety, and performance into an efficient, robust program.

Chapter 8. C++ in Action: Real-World Use-Cases of High-Security Applications

C has long been touted as the backbone of system development and has found considerable utility in creating high-security applications. Proven to be highly efficient as well as flexible, it stands as a cornerstone in the realm of secure programming. This section showcases various real-world examples highlighting the application of C in crafting highly secure structures.

8.1. Fostering Efficiency: Operating Systems

One of the most significant domains where C proves its mettle in building high-security platforms is with Operating Systems. Major operating systems depend on C for their core development. Windows, for instance, is largely written in C, and so are many UNIX and Linux systems. These systems require high-speed processing and increased security, two aspects C fulfills quite efficiently.

The primary reason behind this is the degree of low-level system access offered by C++. It permits direct manipulation of hardware and memory, a feature not available in many higher-level languages. Such abilities make it a suitable choice for developing specialized applications demanding stringent security.

8.2. Protecting the Virtual Space: Security Software

A thriving domain where C++

is extensively utilized is writing various kinds of security software. Antiviruses, for instance, use C++ to build both the back-end scanning engines and the front-end interface. Specifically, security software needs to perform several tasks like file scanning, network protection, and system analysis, all at high speeds.

C allows these applications to run efficiently without consuming too many resources, thus ensuring a seamless user experience. An example here is the Symantec Norton Antivirus, heavily written in C, which provides robust protection against malicious software.

8.3. Secure Transactions: Banking Systems

C++ also plays a vital role in the realm of banking and finance, facilitating secure transactions. It is commonly used to develop financial technology including high-speed trading systems, real-time market data software, and banking software. Its flexibility and performance are what makes it a preferred choice for these applications where speed is crucial.

For example, Poplar - a high-performance framework for building banking systems, primarily uses C++. It facilitates thousands of transactions per minute, ensuring robust performance and secure, encrypted handling of sensitive customer data.

8.4. Shield for Privacy: Blockchain and Cryptography

The world of cybersecurity has also seen the effective implementation of C. Blockchain systems, forming the backbone of cryptocurrencies, use this language for secure and efficient transaction handling. Bitcoin, Ethereum, and other primary digital currencies have their core codebase in C.

Cryptographic systems often need close-to-hardware solutions to work efficiently, which is where C comes into play. Cryptography libraries such as Crypto provide comprehensive functionalities for cryptographic operations. These libraries facilitate essential encryption tools, necessary for maintaining privacy and security.

C also aids in the rapid and secure development of cryptographic algorithms. A great example is the creation of RSA (Rivest-Shamir-Adleman), a widely-used public-key encryption algorithm, using C. It underscores not just the speed but also the security offered by the language.

8.5. Gaming Industry: Combating Cheating Systems

The proliferation of online games has brought with it an increase in cheating provisions, thus demanding secure gaming environments. C++ serves as the primary development language for most gaming engines due to its speed and efficiency.

C also gives developers the tools to actively counter cheating attempts. Anti-cheat software such as Valve's 'Anti-Cheat System' and Epic Games' 'Easy Anti-Cheat' utilize C to effectively detect and prevent cheating, thus ensuring fair play and secure environments for gamers.

C++'s ability to interact with system hardware and networking stack allows these anti-cheat systems to scrutinize and control the game integrity effectively.

In conclusion, the robust features of C allow it to address various dimensions of high-security application programming. C enables programmers to build system-level applications, antiviruses, banking systems, cryptographic algorithms, and even anti-cheat software for video games. The examples highlighted in this section emphasize the robust importance of C++ in delivering both secure and efficient applications across diverse fields.

Chapter 9. Rust in Practice: Real-World Use-Cases of High-Performance Systems

High-performance systems and applications rarely exist in a vacuum — they're the result of clear objectives, resourceful planning, and astute execution of programming technologies. As Rust emerges to be a force to be reckoned with, it's worth examining some of the compelling ways it's been utilized in real-world scenarios to foster secure, high-performance systems. This comprehensive discussion will cover some exemplary Rust use cases and analyze how it lends robustness and efficiency to the systems it powers.

9.1. The Emergence of Rust: An Engine for WebAssembly

Although relatively new, Rust has made its mark in WebAssembly, an open standard that promotes the execution of web applications in a safe, efficient way. Mozilla, Rust's parental organization, was instrumental in the WebAssembly (Wasm) project, and so Rust became one of the first languages to offer robust, inbuilt support for it. Together, Rust and Wasm create a symbiosis that powers high-performance systems on the web.

Rust's powerful async programming model, sophisticated type system, and first-class WASM support are attractive for high-throughput web applications. For instance, 'yew', a Rust-based framework, leverages WASM for building concurrent web apps. The combination of Rust and WASM enables this framework to achieve a high level of performance - faster execution time and supremely low memory footprint.

9.2. Rust and Game Development

Rust has shown significant potential in high-performance game development. It offers the high-level abstractions of modern programming languages while maintaining the power and control of a low-level language like C++.

The `amethyst` project, a data-oriented game engine, exemplifies the integration of Rust in game development. The engine built using Rust makes full use of hardware concurrency and minimizes the chances of runtime errors, resulting in a more reliable and performant game engine. The language's in-built memory safety rules and powerful abstractions make Rust an laudable choice for game developers.

9.3. Bridging the Messaging Gap: Rust + Kafka

Apache Kafka is a high-throughput distributed messaging system utilized by thousands of companies. The need for a fast, reliable Kafka client led to the creation of `rdkafka-rust`, a Rust client for Apache Kafka that provides robust, efficient, and safe bindings.

Rust has shown significant value in bridging the gap between the high-speed traffic of Kafka and the need for ensuring reliable message delivery. Thanks to Rust's zero-cost abstractions, `rdkafka-rust` can offer both high performance and high-level programming constructs that make integrating Kafka in high-demand systems less daunting.

9.4. Redefining Operating Systems with Rust: The Redox OS Case

Operating systems (OS) need to be incredibly stable and secure, and

Rust's unique philosophy makes it a superb fit. Redox OS stands as a testament to Rust's prowess. It's a Unix-like OS written in Rust that aims to bring improved safety and protection to a domain traditionally dominated by C/C++.

Through Rust's constructs, Redox OS ensures memory safety without garbage collection, handles system-level concurrency without data races, and includes other Rust advantages like small binary sizes and massive libraries. As a result, Redox OS takes strides in the direction of secure, highly reliable operating systems.

9.5. Rust in Browser Engines: Servo Project

Rust sure makes its presence known in the realm of browser engines. Mozilla's Servo Project, a prototype web browser engine, and is an excellent showcase of Rust's ability to power complex, performance-driven systems. Leveraging the security benefits of Rust, Servo hopes to provide faster, safer browsing experiences.

With Rust, Servo achieves parallelized layout and rendering, and safely handles component complexity. Servo's design reveals the impressive capability of Rust in creating high-security, high-performance systems in the browser engine domain.

In summary, Rust's trajectory in transforming high-performance systems is notable. Whether powering the next generation of web applications, buttressing high-performing game engines, facilitating reliable distributed messaging, revolutionizing operating systems, or advancing web browser engines, Rust proves instrumental in developing remarkably efficient, high-security solutions. This discussion crystallizes Rust's illuminating application across a range of domains and underpins its vital role in shaping the future of high-performance computing.

Chapter 10. Choosing Between C++ and Rust: Factors to Consider

When it comes to selecting a programming language for a particular project, multiple factors come into play, which can significantly influence the final decision. Both C and Rust have unique offerings that vary greatly, hence different projects will benefit more from one over the other depending on their specific requirements. In this analysis, we will delve into significant factors that you should consider when choosing between C and Rust, making it easier for you to land a decision which ensures optimal project success.

10.1. Learning Curve

Both C and Rust are not among the easiest languages to pick up, especially for a beginner. C, while being older and featuring more abundant learning resources, has one of the steepest learning curves among all programming languages. This complexity comes from the extensive feature-set it provides, which includes a blend of procedural, object-oriented, and generic programming features. These overlapping features often make it difficult to grasp the language's full potential without an ample amount of time and practice.

Rust, on the other hand, encapsulates a different type of complexity. While it intended to be more readable and maintainable, its uniqueness lies in its memory safety guarantees without a garbage collector, along with a few other advanced features. These unique features often involve new programming concepts to learn and grasp, thereby influencing the learning curve of the language.

Whether one should go for simplicity or the necessity to explore more complex features at the cost of a steep learning curve is a decision that should align with the project requirements and the experience level of the development team.

10.2. Safety and Security

Security forms the backbone of most systems today and often is a decisive factor in choosing a programming language.

C++ has faced substantial criticism due to its lack of built-in memory safety, leading to prevalent vulnerabilities such as buffer overflows and null pointer dereferencing bugs.

Rust counters this by providing memory safety guarantees without a garbage collector's cost. It employs a unique mechanism of ownership with a system of borrowing and lifetimes to ensure a high level of memory safety. This built-in mechanism can eliminate a variety of common programming errors, leading to more secure and stable applications, which is particularly useful for system-level programming.

If ensuring high system stability and security is paramount for your project, Rust's memory safety feature provides a robust advantage over C++.

10.3. Efficiency and Performance

Performance is another crucial factor when choosing between C++, a proven performer known for its fine-grained control over system resources, and Rust, acclaimed for competitive runtime performance.

While both C and Rust compile to machine code, giving similar possibilities of manual optimization, their design philosophies slightly differ. C provides you with a low-level touch in managing memory, which means it can leverage the hardware to its fullest capacity. Consequently, it enables efficient memory management, fast execution, and higher control over system resources, making it suitable for high-frequency and high-performance computing applications.

Rust, while aiming for a similar level of control and performance as C++, brings in safety and concurrency as a part of its design. It ensures that as much of the heavy lifting as possible is completed at compile-time, leading to efficient runtime performance. Its primary focus on safety doesn't let it compromise on power or control.

Therefore, while both languages exhibit robust performance characteristics, the right choice will depend on the level of system resource control required and the development team's skill in harnessing these language features.

10.4. System-level Programming

Programming applications close to the system hardware is where both languages capture their primary use and target audience.

C++ has been the go-to language for system-level programming for decades due to its feature-set allowing high control over system resources. Its object-oriented nature combined with generic programming features make it an excellent choice for building efficient, flexible, and powerful system applications.

Rust, thanks to its focus on memory safety and concurrency, is also well-designed for system-level programming. It allows for low-level control comparable to C++, but its added safety and modern syntax make it less error-prone. It pitches itself as an efficient language for creating reliable system software.

If you need to do system-level programming, it is crucial to consider the required level of control over system resources, language familiarity, memory safety, and concurrency management.

10.5. Community and Ecosystem

The size and activity level of a language's community and ecosystem can significantly impact its usage, growth, and support for libraries and tools.

C, being older and widely adopted, enjoys a gigantic community, with every imaginable library and tool available. The C Standard Library and Boost, among many others, offer extensive capabilities that can significantly accelerate application development.

Rust's ecosystem, while younger, is rapidly growing and maturing. Its standard library is not as expansive as C, but many high-quality crates are available for use. Rust's package manager, cargo, allows for easy dependency management, testing, and building. While the Rust community is also notably helpful and friendly, its size and available resources do not yet match C.

Choosing between C and Rust vis-à-vis ecosystem and community support involves balancing between the abundance of resources in C and the ease of use provided by more modern tools and a rapidly growing community in Rust.

To wrap up, scrutinizing over these factors based on the specific requirements of your project should guide you in deciding between C++ and Rust. Remember that the ultimate goal is to select a language that will help deliver a successful and efficient project rather than sticking to personal language preferences. Let the project's needs guide your decision, and you will find success in the form of a robust, efficient, and secure system.

Chapter 11. The Future of High-Security, High-Performance Systems with C++ and Rust

In an era of accelerated digital transformation, the stakes for securing system performance have never been higher. The twin linchpins here are C++ and Rust, two programming languages that play an instrumental role - both owing to their unique strengths, as well as their evolving capabilities.

11.1. The Ongoing Reign of C++

C++ has had a long-standing reign in the realm of high-performance computing, primarily due to its granular control over system resources and efficient code execution. It has furnished programmers with the ability to fine-tune their applications, squeeze every bit of performance from hardware, and thereby, influence the speed of execution.

C++ provides extensive control over memory management. It allows for manual memory management, ensuring that developers can be precise about how and when memory is allocated and freed. This feature plays a crucial role in high-performance computing, where efficient memory management can significantly affect performance.

Moreover, C++ comes loaded with a robust Standard Template Library (STL), which provides an array of pre-built classes for various data structures and algorithms. This library can optimise code execution and save precious development time.

However, considering the level of authority it gives, C++ demands a high degree of expertise and vigilance. A small oversight in memory management can lead to bugs and security vulnerabilities, and the complex nature of STL can sometimes overshadow its benefits.

11.2. The Rise of Rust

Enter Rust, a relatively new language focusing on performance and safety, notably safe concurrency. Rust provides memory safety without using a garbage collector, which sets it apart.

Rust ensures memory safety through its unique take on pointers and ownership. Each value in Rust has a variable known as its "owner", and there can only be one owner at a time. When the owner goes out of scope, the value will be automatically cleaned up. This system effectively eliminates a large swath of system bugs, including the infamous null and dangling pointers, without affecting performance.

Additionally, Rust is designed to help programmers manage concurrent programming safely. Data races are one of the toughest bugs to track down in concurrent programming. Rust's ownership system inherently provides a mechanism to prevent data races at compile time, making concurrent programming more accessible and less error-prone.

Despite these admired safety features, Rust requires a steep learning curve. The stringent compiler with its complex rules to enforce safety at compile time may confound beginners and experienced developers alike.

11.3. Comparing C++ and Rust for High-Performance Systems

Both languages have their unique strengths. C++, with its fine-grained control over system resources, has unmatched performance. On the other hand, Rust, with its focus on memory safety and safe concurrency, provides high performance without the risks typically associated with system level programming.

A study on GitHub's top repositories provides insights on how these languages are used. C++ shines in areas such as operating system development, game programming, and real-time systems. Meanwhile, Rust is found carving a niche in system utilities, game engines, and increasingly, web assembly applications.

Given the ongoing development and extraordinary community support, C++ will continue to be relevant in building high-performance systems. However, if the trends are anything to go by, Rust, with its focus on safety and concurrency, will gain more acceptance. The choice between the two languages would rely heavily on the specific needs of the system and the expertise of the development team.

11.4. The Path Forward: Combining Strengths?

Perhaps the future does not need to be an "either/or" scenario between C++ and Rust. Maybe it involves leveraging each language's strengths in a symbiotic relationship that enriches the system's overall integrity and performance.

Rust's ability to interoperate with C code opens up possibilities for using Rust for portioning code requiring high security or concurrency, while using C to handle parts needing extreme performance. Some large companies, like Microsoft and Mozilla, have already started encouraging this practice in their projects. For many developers, the prospect of blending the performance of C++ with the safety of Rust provides an exciting avenue for the development of high-security, high-performance systems.

In conclusion, the future seems bright. While C++ will continue to fortify systems with its proven performance and control, Rust is expected to find its way into more applications, ensuring safety without compromising performance. These developments promise to collectively raise the bar for the security and performance of high-performance systems.

www.ingramcontent.com/pod-product-compliance
Lightning Source LLC
La Vergne TN
LVHW051633050326
832903LV00033B/4740

* 9 7 9 8 8 5 6 0 5 9 1 2 9 *